Leicester's
A VICTORIA

To Sid and Ann,
with all good wishes,

Derek.

The Town Hall, Town Hall Square, adjacent to Horsefair Street, Leicester (Eugene Dowds)

Derek Seaton

The painting of the Town Hall,
on the front cover, is the work of
Douglas Smith local architect and
artist and features in his book
Leicester: Painting and sketches
published in 2001

The photograph of the frozen
fountain, on the rear cover,
was taken by the author
on 13 December 1991

Published by Leicester City Council 2004
Designed by Kim Pereira, Creativity Works.

ISBN 1 901156 23 0

Winged Assyrian lions guard the Fountain in Town Hall Square (Derek Seaton)

PREFACE

The growth of population, in Leicester, during the 19th century was quite dramatic. The first National Census of 1801 recorded 16,953 people living in the town, the majority of whom were employed in the hosiery industry. One hundred years later, when the census of 1901 was taken, the population had increased to 211,579. By this time 26,491 of its citizens were employed in the manufacturing of boots and shoes whilst 12,389 people continued to earn their living in the hosiery trade. From a small hosiery town in 1801, Leicester had expanded into a huge and diverse industrialised centre.

One of the fundamental problems which the Leicester Corporation had to address, during the massive expansion of the town and its population, in the 19th century, was the pressing need to build a new Town Hall in order to administer, effectively, a wide range of services to cope with the growing and changing needs of the Borough. What eventually emerged was a much-loved municipal building, which, together with its tranquil square and fountain, proudly demonstrated the civic pride of Victorian Leicester.

It has been a privilege to be invited to produce this book and I am indebted to a number of people who have so very kindly given of their time and knowledge, without which I could not have written *Leicester's Town Hall: A Victorian Jewel*.

I am very grateful indeed to the Lord Mayor of Leicester, Councillor Ramnik Kavia for his kindness in writing the Foreword, to Douglas Smith for generously allowing me to use his wonderful painting of the Town Hall and to Virginia Wright, Blue Badge Guide, for kindly proof-reading the manuscript. Also to Jack Collinson, former Assistant Town Clerk, for his personal recollections of the night when the Town Hall received a direct hit during an enemy air raid.

Grateful acknowledgement is also made to the Lord Mayor's Secretariat for their assistance and encouragement with special thanks to Diane Batson who typed the manuscript and provided me with unfailing support throughout the project. Nick Carter, Editor of the *Leicester Mercury*, for his permission to use a number of photographs from the newspaper's archives and to Steve England and his colleagues at the *Leicester Mercury* library for enabling me to have access to files and photographs relating to the Town Hall.

I am also indebted to Ben Beazley, J.D. Bennett, Keith Dickens, Alexandra Dowds and Malcolm Tovey for their important contributions.

Finally, if I have, inadvertently, omitted anyone from the acknowledgements please accept my apology. You can be assured of my gratitude.

Derek Seaton
January 2004

CONTENTS

Chapter One: Time for change

Prior to the building of Leicester's present Town Hall (1874-1876), the Borough Corporation held their meetings in the 14th century Guildhall situated in St Martin's Church Lane, later to become Town Hall Lane and now Guildhall Lane. The Guildhall was built by the Gild of Corpus Christi, which was founded in 1343, and was used by the Mayor and members of the Town Council for their meetings from 1495 onwards. The building was purchased by the Corporation in 1563 for the sum of £25.15s.4d.

The Guildhall, now a Grade I listed building, was to serve as the Borough's Town Hall for a continuous period of 381 years. In January 1836, the Guildhall also became the Town's first police station upon the creation of the Leicester Borough Police Force following the passing of the Municipal Corporations Act 1835. The new force was commanded by Frederick Goodyear, who was appointed as Superintendent of Police and Head Constable and consisted of 5 sergeants and 45 constables. In addition to the setting up of the force's headquarters at the Guildhall, a charge room and three cells were created on the ground floor of the east wing.

As early as 1814 it was considered that the Guildhall was too small to be able to cope, efficiently, in meeting the needs of the rapidly expanding town. A local architect and surveyor William Firmadge, who was Mayor of Leicester in 1809, was invited to draw up plans for a new Town Hall. Whilst the need for new Municipal Buildings and Courts of Justice was felt to be a pressing requirement, by many members of the Town Council, the question of whether a large public hall should be incorporated in the plans led to fierce debates taking place and no firm conclusion was reached.

The account for the design work by Firmadge was eventually paid on 1 May 1820 but the Corporation took no further action for the next fifty years.

One who took up the crusade for the building of a new Town Hall was Alderman John Biggs who was elected to the newly-formed Corporation on 26 December 1835. From 1845 onwards, Alderman Biggs, a local hosiery manufacturer, together with his younger brother Alderman William Biggs were the leading campaigners. They were prominent members of the powerful local Liberal Party and both served as Mayor of the Borough on three occasions. John was Mayor in 1840, 1847 and 1855 whilst William held the civic office in 1842, 1848 and again in 1859.

Alderman John Biggs was elected to Parliament, to represent the Borough, in 1856, 1857 and 1859, and Alderman William Biggs was the Liberal Member of Parliament for Newport, Isle of Wight from 1852 to 1857.

Both were ardent supporters, during their influential years, of what they saw as a pressing need for new Municipal Buildings as Leicester developed from a small market town into a large urbanised area.

The Portrait of John Biggs, Council Chamber, Town Hall, Leicester (Lord Mayor's Secretariat)

At a meeting of the Town Council, on 20 December 1870, it was resolved that "Municipal Buildings were absolutely required for the convenient transaction of public business." Members were almost equally divided upon two available sites. One was occupied by a property in nearby Friar Lane and the second possibility was the cattle market area situated in Horsefair Street. The Friar Lane site contained a council owned building, the property had been purchased by the Corporation in 1866 and was formerly owned by Beaumont Burnaby, a solicitor and Registrar of the Prebendal Court of St Margaret's, Leicester who died in 1848.

Plans had been approved for a new cattle market to be built, in Aylestone Road, in 1871 and was due to be opened in the spring of 1872, thus releasing the central site in Horsefair Street.

On 17 January 1871, the Town Council took the decision to erect the Municipal Buildings in Friar Lane and a committee was appointed to be responsible for the scheme. The cost of the buildings, which would not include a large hall, was to be met within a budget of £25,000 exclusive of the furniture.

Prizes of £200, £100 and £50 were offered for the three best competitive designs and George Edmund Street, the well-known English ecclesiastical and domestic architect was appointed to assess the designs submitted and to select five from which the Council could choose the final three and award the prizes. Some thirty-nine entries were received and, on

Horsefair Street in 1868. Directly opposite the wagon is the old Cattle Market (Leicester Mercury)

11 July 1871, the Corporation made their choice from the five selected, with some suggested modifications, by George Edmund Street and awarded the prizes as follows:

First	Barnard and Smith	Leicester (£200)
Second	Goddard and Spiers	Leicester (£100)
Third	Innocent and Brown	Sheffield (£50)

Problems then arose when the Municipal Buildings Committee asked the award-winning architects to reconsider their designs "with reference to Mr Street's objections and suggestions of the Committee". Whilst Goddard and Spiers and Innocent and Brown were willing to do so, the Leicester architects Thomas Barnard and William Beaumont Smith were not prepared to reconsider their designs. On 26 October 1871, the Committee recommended the adoption of the plans by Goddard and Spiers.

The decision was immediately challenged by those Council members who had preferred the alternative site in Horsefair Street and the motion to adopt the report was met by an amendment to the effect that the Municipal Buildings Committee had exceeded its powers by requiring the three firms of architects to enter into a further competition. The amendment also called for the whole question to be referred to a Committee of the entire Council. The amendment was carried by 31 to 21 votes.

The three members of the Municipal Buildings Committee who had conferred with the architects - Alderman Alfred Burgess, Alderman George Toller and Alderman George Stevenson felt that the Resolution of the Council cast a slur on their reputations and proceeded to resign their seats as Aldermen of the Borough. Matters were quickly resolved, after explanations were given by the mover and seconder and others who supported the resolution, and the three Aldermen were re-elected at a meeting of the Town Council on 9 November 1871. The resolution adopting the Friar Lane site was finally rescinded in September 1872 and steps were taken for the new Municipal Buildings to be erected on the site of the old cattle market in Horsefair Street, which had been cleared following the opening of the new cattle market, in Aylestone Road, on 6 April 1872.

A new design competition was advertised which resulted in twenty-five architects submitting their plans for the proposed buildings which were not to exceed £30,000 and the prizes for the best three designs were to be identical to the 1871 competition. The Corporation appointed Thomas Henry Wyatt, the President of the Royal Institute of British Architects, of 77 Great Russell Street, London, to select five from ten of the competitive designs "for the ultimate choice of three by the Council".

The five sets of plans chosen by Thomas Wyatt in his report to the Town Council, dated 5 July 1873, were (in alphabetical order):

Goddard and Spiers

Francis John Hames

Ordish and Traylen

Scott Brothers (G.G.Scott and J.D. Scott)

Robert Stark Wilkinson

The design for Leicester's new Town Hall submitted by Goddard and Spiers (Leicester City Council)

A special meeting of the Town Council was held, on 22 July 1873, at the old Town Hall to consider Thomas Wyatt's report. Every councillor had received a copy of the report and the task was to choose the winning design from the five entries selected by Wyatt.

It was agreed that the decision should be arrived at by ballot and the councillors would vote against the design they favoured least! Alderman John Stafford suggested that: "they strike out one each time." The result of the balloting was reported in the *Leicester Advertiser* (26 July 1873) and was as follows:

	Wilkinson	Scott Bros	Goddard & Spiers	Hames	Ordish & Traylen
1st ballot	25	2	16	4	0
2nd ballot		13	22	8	5
3rd ballot		20		12	16
4th ballot				19	29

Thus, the design by Francis John Hames which finally, on the fourth ballot, attracted the fewest number of votes *against* became the winner of the competition.

This unusual method of deciding upon the winning design was commented upon, at some length in *The Notes of the Week* column in the *Leicester Chronicle and The Leicestershire Mercury* (26 July 1873):

"The names of the competitors were placed in a list and each member of the Council was required to vote (by ballot) against the competitor to whom he was most opposed." The article referred to the competing architects being blackballed.

The columnist went on: "Ordinarily when men make a choice they proceed on the principle for what they *like best*. The Town Council of Leicester, in a most important matter, makes its selection by voting against, so Mr Hames' designs were carried because he had the fewest votes in the Municipal Body."

"Why was the question not tested on the opposite principle - that of common sense and fairness - by an appeal to the members of the Council to vote positively for all of the competitors and to award the palm to him who had the largest number of votes in his favour?"

Nevertheless, no satisfactory explanation was given, the decision had been made, albeit in a bizarre fashion, the prizes had been awarded and Francis Hames had been chosen to undertake the prestigious commission.

The result of the competition was confirmed by the Borough Council on 22 July 1873:

First Prize	Francis John Hames	London	(£200)
Second Prize	Ordish and Traylen	Leicester	(£100)
Third Prize	George Gilbert Scott Jnr and John Oldrid Scott	London	(£50)

(The Scotts were brothers and the sons of Sir George Gilbert Scott, RA)

Francis John Hames, whose plans emerged as the winning design, was born at 1 Haymarket, Leicester on 2 June 1849. He was the second son of Francis Hames and Mary Hames (née Angrave). Francis Hames senior was a saddler and harness maker who also owned horses for hire.

The young Francis Hames had received his training as a student architect from William Millican an architect and surveyor of Leicester who became a Borough Councillor and, coincidentally, the Chairman of the Municipal Buildings Committee. At the time he was awarded the commission, Francis Hames resided at 49 Woburn Place, London and his office was located at 40 Chancery Lane in the metropolis.

Whilst working in London he met a fellow-architect, William Eden Nesfield who, between 1868 and 1874, was working on the construction of the great house at Kinmel Park, Denbighshire (now Clwyd). Kinmel Park was the first large nineteenth century house to be built in the Queen Anne style. Hames was introduced to this distinctive style of architecture by William Nesfield with whom he worked until 1872.

The plans by Hames for the building of Leicester's Town Hall were quite revolutionary in the sense that many of his contempories, involved in the erection and construction of late 19th century Town Halls, chose the popular styles of the day - namely Classical or Neo-Gothic in design. Francis Hames decided to build in the Queen Anne style using brick rather than stone. He described his choice of style as being: "Traditional in character rather than strictly in adherence to the style; yet traces can be seen of the time of Queen Anne and the Hotel de Ville in France".

At a meeting of the Town Council, on 30 September 1873, a report from the Municipal Buildings Committee was considered. It was agreed that: "the buildings may be completed for the sum of £30,000", this was based upon an estimate prepared by Franklin Andrews, a firm of surveyors at 5 Adelaide Place, London Bridge. The Committee was authorised: "to instruct Mr Hames to proceed to carry out his awarded designs."

One of the earlier, influential advocates of the new Municipal Buildings, Alderman John Biggs, sadly was not destined to see the realisation of his dream. He died in Leicester, on 4 June 1871, aged 70 years, but his presence lingered on in the form of a statue, the cost of which was met by public subscription and was, appropriately, unveiled during 1873, the year in which the decision was taken to build the new Town Hall.

John Biggs was so well-known even following his demise, that in the days of the trams passengers could board one on the far side of

The Chambers at 40-43 Chancery Lane, Holborn where Francis Hames had his office (Derek Seaton)

Statue of John Biggs, Welford Place, Leicester (Derek Seaton)

The vacant site, which was formerly occupied by the Cattle Market, looking across to Bishop Street in 1874 (Leicester City Council)

the city, announce to the conductor "John Biggs" and be safely deposited in Welford Place.

Francis Hames, having revised his drawings in consultation with members of the Municipal Buildings Committee, was ready to commence and, on 15 December 1873, a report regarding the advertising for tenders for executing the earthworks was considered at a meeting of the Town Council. The tender for the foundations submitted by Flude and White, in the sum of £429, was accepted.

Within the next three months tenders were received from eight building contractors and, on 3 March 1874, the Council awarded the contract to William Brass of 47 Old Street, St Luke's, London who submitted the lowest tender at £31,935. The actual price of the tender was: "£31,285 plus £650 extra if the whole of the external stonework was in Ketton stone rather than part Bath and part Ketton stone."

The plans did not allow for a public hall to be included as this was not felt to be necessary. In 1874, public meetings in Leicester usually took place at Thomas Cook's Temperance Hall, in Granby Street, which was built in 1853 and could accommodate 1800 people.

Francis Hames decided to build his Town Hall in Suffolk brick rather than the popular local Leicester red brick. Having resolved to dress the entire external masonry with Ketton stone, from the quarry in nearby Rutland, he chose Caen stone for his designs for the interior stonework.

The foundation stone of the new Town Hall was laid by the Mayor, Alderman William Kempson, on Monday 3 August 1874, one of the first Bank Holiday Mondays to be enjoyed by the workers of the town. The ceremony commenced "at Three o'clock precisely and the Military Band and the Royal Corps Band were in attendance." The bands played "Rule Britannia" whilst the stone was adjusted. In accordance with ancient custom, the Freemasons "tried the stone" with a level and plumb rule. The Mayor then used the mallet and declared the stone well and truly laid, following which the bands played "God Save the Queen." Afterwards, the Mayor and his guests adjourned to the Corn Exchange for a celebratory luncheon.

*The Temperance Hall,
Granby Street, Leicester
(The Thomas Cook Archives)*

The laying of the foundation stone (Leicester Mercury)

The foundation stone
(Derek Seaton)

The work of the stonemason is shown, in great detail, on both sides of the foundation stone. The rising sun, to the right, sheds its warmth on clover, mushrooms and sunflowers whilst a duck wings its way overhead. Night, to the left, is illustrated by a crescent moon with a face, poppies, whose seeds induce sleep, with an owl, in full flight, surveying the scene.

A representative party of schoolchildren, accompanied by their teachers, attended the ceremony and were invited to "tea at the Temperance Hall at 4 o'clock."

Further items of expenditure were agreed by the Council as the work progressed and modifications and additional features were decided upon. These included:

Formation of a Club Room in the roof	£230
Extra Finishings	£148
Portland Cement in the Front Waiting Hall and Ground Floor Corridors	£313
Accommodation for the Fire Brigade and Lamp Lighters	£600
Enlargement to the Tower	£1,785

The intention was that the building would be completed during 1875 but a series of setbacks resulted in the construction work proceeding well into 1876. Firstly, the clerk of works Reuben Beaver, who was a Leicester builder and contractor, resigned from his all-important position. His resignation was reported at a meeting of the Borough Council on 28 July 1874. The then vacant post was advertised in *The Builder* and the local newspapers. Thirty-six applications were received and five candidates were selected for interview which resulted in a Mr Vicars being appointed at a wage of £3.3s.0d a week, an increase of 13 shillings per week over his predecessor!

In June 1875 the bricklayers went on strike for higher wages. The winter of 1875-6 was extremely severe and, as a result of continual heavy frosts, the work came to an abrupt halt.

Finally, in May 1876 the painters decided to strike, in an effort to secure higher wages and shorter working hours, which further delayed the completion of the building.

At a meeting of the Town Council on 30 March 1876 it was agreed that the title of the new Municipal Buildings should be the Town Hall.

The new Town Hall nearing completion in 1876. Note the Cattle Market buildings in the foreground (Leicester City Council)

The Town Councillors outside the new
Town Hall following the opening ceremony
(Leicester City Council)

The Silver Key used by Alderman Barfoot to
officially open the Town Hall
(Lord Mayor's Secretariat)

The official opening of the new Town Hall took place on Monday 7 August 1876. Once again a Bank Holiday Monday was chosen and the town celebrated in great style. In an air of festive mood, the streets were decorated with banners and bunting; flowers were everywhere to be seen and the church bells pealed. Following the formal closure of the old Town Hall, a grand civic procession walked from the Guildhall to the new Town Hall where a huge crowd witnessed the official opening performed by the Mayor, Alderman William Barfoot.

Saddle horses were hired for the occasion from Francis Hames senior, the father of the architect of the Town Hall, for the use of the Head Constable Joseph Farndale and twelve of his officers at a cost of £3.7s.6d.

After the ceremony, a short Council meeting took place followed by a Civic Dinner held in the Corn Exchange. The citizens of Leicester enjoyed a celebratory firework display, in the evening, on Victoria Park and the Mayor's Ball took place in the Assembly Rooms (now the City Rooms) to conclude a memorable day in the Town's history.

The total cost of the building amounted to £52,911.2s.8d, considerably more than the original estimate but Francis Hames had achieved the distinction of having created the first large civic building in England to be built in the Queen Anne style. The frontage of the Town Hall measured 216 feet in length and with two wings which extended up Bishop Street and Horsefair Street to Bowling Green Street formed three sides of a quadrangle the width being 118 feet. The slight slope of the ground added to the pleasing appearance of the front elevation of the building.

Leicester's new Town Hall contained a number of outstanding features. Undoubtedly, the finest room in the building was the Council Chamber. It measured 56 feet by 32 feet and the most prominent feature was the semicircular plaster ceiling which was decorated with flowers and contained the Arms of the Borough of Leicester. This ornate and beautiful ceiling was a superb example of the skills of Victorian craftsmen.

The original Council Chamber (The Builder)

The stained glass window showing Alderman Gabriel Newton with a green-coat schoolboy (Eugene Dowds)

Stained glass featured in the Council Chamber and the small public waiting hall. The contractors for the stained glass were Heaton, Butler and Bayne, Garrick Street, London. Individual panes of glass, in the Council Chamber, contained the names and initials of each respective Mayor since the passing of the Municipal Corporations Act 1835 together with the date of their election to office. The work was executed, according to the architect's designs, at a cost of £299.0s.0d.

The furniture was purchased from Gillow and Company of London for £736.4s.0d. and elegant purpose made brass chandeliers were installed by Richardson,Ellson and Company, London in the sum of £230.7s.0d.

Attractive external lamps and wrought iron brackets, which cost £180.0s.0d, were the work of Frederick Webb, ironmonger, gasfitter, electric bell hanger and tinplate worker, 45 High Street, Leicester.

The six large stained glass windows placed in the waiting room, looking into Bowling Green Street, depicted important historical figures with Leicestershire connections - Simon de Montfort, Bishop Hugh Latimer, John O'Gaunt, Sir Thomas White, William Wyggeston and Alderman Gabriel Newton.

Alderman Gabriel Newton, a local woolcomber, who was Mayor of Leicester in 1732, used the greater part of his fortune for the clothing and education of poor boys in Leicester and several other places. This great benefactor founded the Alderman Newton School in Leicester, where the boys wore distinctive green jackets.

Accommodation and amenities were provided for the use of the Alderman and Councillors plus the officials of the Town Council. An important feature was the courts which consisted of a Principal or Crown Court measuring 58 feet by 36 feet and a Second or Nisi Prius Court 38 feet by 30 feet. In addition there were rooms for the Judges,

Magistrates and Barristers.

Importantly, there was a new headquarters for the Borough Police Force which included a muster room (56 feet by 32 feet) and a storeroom plus thirteen cells - eight for male and five for female prisoners, together with a narrow parade ground, at the

The Principal Court (Leicester Mercury)

rear of the cells, where the prisoners could be exercised. The accommodation was urgently required to replace the totally inadequate police station which had been housed at the Guildhall since the force was founded in 1836.

In addition, a small fire station was built to accommodate the Borough's Fire Brigade headed by John Johnson who had been appointed Superintendent on 13 February 1872 upon the formation of the Brigade. The fire station was situated towards the Horsefair Street end of Bowling Green Street.

The Brigade's equipment consisted of two horse-drawn manually operated engines and a horse-drawn steam powered engine, a workshop and a drying room for the hoses plus a muster room for twenty firemen. A major problem arose from the fact that the Brigade did not own any horses at this point thus, in times of emergency, frantic searches had to be made of the nearby streets to locate horses, owned by the Corporation for drawing refuse carts etc, which could be commandeered and taken to the fire station in order to speedily harness them to the waiting fire engines!

The plans included: "A commodious house for the Superintendent of the Brigade" (*Spencer's Illustrated Leicester Almanack 1877*). Superintendent Johnson's residence was at 4 Bowling Green Street and was known as Fire Engine House.

Additional resources, incorporated in the plans, consisted of a mortuary, rooms for the Inspector of Nuisances and a six-roomed house for the Head Constable at the corner of Bishop Street and Bowling Green Street. Joseph Farndale was the Head Constable (1871-1882) followed by James Duns (1882-1894).

The Head Constable's house conveniently overlooked the parade ground situated at the rear of the building. The parade ground was paved with four inch granite sets, covering an area of 760 square yards, which could also be used by the firemen to clean their engines and dry their hose reels. Acting upon the advice of the Watch committee, sleeping accommodation was allowed for 30 Lamplighters in addition to a Lamplighters' muster room, a store and workroom for the repairing of lamps.

There was also an apartment provided for the Town Hall Keeper and Crier of Courts, a post to which John White was appointed in 1876. He was a former constable in the Borough Police Force which he left, in November 1872, to become the Town Hall Keeper at the old Town Hall in Town Hall Lane.

Visitors to Leicester are frequently surprised to discover that its major civic building bears conflicting dates. The gable on the front elevation shows 1875, whereas the wrought-iron gates at the main entrance, situated immediately underneath, gives 1876 as the year of completion. Serious delays which occurred during the construction of the building, and which have been described earlier, resulted in the Town Hall opening a year later than originally scheduled in the building programme.

Gable on the front elevation (Eugene Dowds)

Main entrance (Eugene Dowds)

The Latin inscription above the front entrance
(Derek Seaton)

A unique characteristic incorporated into Leicester's Town Hall was the Latin inscription carved in the stonework, over the main entrance, at the front of the building. The inscription reads: *NISI DOMINUS AEDIFICAVERIT DOMUM FRUSTA LABORAVERUNT QUI AEDFICANT EAM*

It is a biblical quotation from Psalm 127, Authorised Version of the Bible and translates:

Except the Lord build the house
they labour in vain that build it

Despite the series of delays the clock, due to be placed in the 145 ft high oblong tower, at the north end of the building, had not been completed by the time of the official opening owing to the illness of the local clockmaker, Edward Thomas Loseby, whose tender of £907.0s.0d. had been accepted. The new Town Hall stood without its clock for the next three years and became the butt of jokes by comedians appearing on the nearby music halls. Eventually, Loseby purchased a movement from John Smith and Sons, Derby and had it installed, at his own expense, purely as a temporary measure. There were five bells, in the cupola, which were cast by Mears and Stainbank of London; the hour bell, which weighed twenty one hundredweight and four smaller bells, ranging from three and a half to seven hundredweight, to strike the quarter hours. The temporary clock mechanism continues to tick on, quite accurately, to this day!

The Town Hall Clock and Tower (Eugene Dowds)

The Fountain in Town Hall Square (Eugene Dowds)

29

Alderman Israel Hart
(Leicester City Council)

The elegant Town Hall Square was also designed by Francis Hames and laid out in 1879 at a cost of £1200. The ornamental fountain which had a central feature in the form of four winged Assyrian lions in bronze painted cast-iron was the generous gift of Alderman Israel Hart, who was High Bailiff in 1879, for which he paid a sum thought to be in the region of £2000. The fountain was erected in a basin (30 feet in diameter and 2 feet 6 inches in depth) and constructed from massive blocks of Shap granite.

Francis Hames successfully incorporated the splendid fountain into the design work for his overall plan for the laying out of the square. (There is an identical fountain in Oporto in Portugal from the same moulds which were later discovered in Paris). Alderman Hart duly unveiled his fountain, on 24 September 1879, during the Mayoralty of Alderman Clement Stretton.

Alderman Hart and his business partner, Joseph Levy, manufactured men's made to measure worsted suits and operated from a large factory in Wimbledon Street, Leicester. The firm of Hart and Levy, Wholesale Tailors and Clothiers, achieved great commercial success through a chain of retail outlets which they established throughout the North of England, the Midlands and East Anglia. Israel Hart was a generous benefactor and donated the first Branch Free Library, in Garendon Street, within the ward he represented in 1883. He became the first member of the Jewish congregation to become Mayor of Leicester in 1884 and again in 1885 and 1886 and for a fourth time in 1893. Alderman Hart was knighted by Queen Victoria in January 1895.

Firemen of the Leicester Borough Fire Brigade pictured with a horse-drawn manual fire engine, at the fire station, in the Town Hall yard circa 1878 (Malcolm Tovey)

Although the fire station, at the rear of the Town Hall, became operational in 1876 it was to be some years before the Brigade acquired its own horse and stabling in the vicinity, as no provision had been made, in the plans, for either beast or shelter.

By 1889 the Corporation acquired a building in Bishop Street and altered it into stables for four horses, two of which were used exclusively by the Fire Brigade. In 1890, Walter Parker was transferred from the Highway and Sewage Department to become the Brigade horse keeper, coachman and fireman at a wage of £1.2s.0d per week. It was his job to look after the horses, put them into their harness on a fire call and drive them to the fire. His service with the Borough Fire Brigade spanned thirty- nine years.

The need for a large fire station quickly became apparent and the Corporation responded by acquiring a site in nearby Rutland Street where a new Central Fire Station was built. The new station, which included stabling for six horses plus a horse keeper's house, was formally opened on 30 August 1892 by the Mayor of Leicester, Alderman Thomas Wright J.P.

In July 1894, Thomas Wilkinson Lumley was appointed Head Constable in succession to James Duns who had resigned on health grounds. The Town Council decided to discontinue the provision of a residence, at the Town Hall, for the Head Constable. At a meeting of the Watch Committee on 15 October 1894, a decision was taken in respect of telephone lines to be laid between the Police Headquarters and the residence of the new Head Constable, Thomas W. Lumley which was at 'Weathersfield', Hinckley Road, Leicester. For a short time the house, formerly occupied by the Head Constable, was used to provide suitable accommodation for the Police Surgeon. By 1895 the house was appropriated as offices for the Rate Clerk, George Rose and his collectors plus additional room for the Leicester School Board.

Alderman Arthur Wakerley
(Leicester City Council)

An important event in Leicester's civic history occurred on 9 November 1897 when Alderman Arthur Wakerley, at the age of thirty-five years, became the town's youngest Mayor in modern times. Alderman Wakerley, an architect and surveyor, joined the Borough Council as a Liberal Councillor in 1886.

During the Mayoralty of Alderman Wakerley, a tragedy occurred at Whitwick Colliery in north west Leicestershire when, on 19 April 1898, a serious gob fire resulted in the deaths of thirty-five men and boys in the mine. This was the worst colliery disaster in the history of the Leicestershire coalfield. Alderman Wakerley was instrumental in the setting up of a Trust Fund to provide financial support for the families of the victims. He was one of the Trustees of the Fund which proved to be vital in coming to the assistance of the 146 dependants of the disaster.

Chapter Two:
Completing the quadrangle

By 1908, the Estate and Burial Grounds Committee reported to the Borough Council that there was "an urgent need for additional and improved accommodation" for both the Education Department and the Borough Police Headquarters. Plans prepared by the original architect of the Town Hall, Francis John Hames together with the Borough Surveyor, Enoch George Mawbey were accepted. Seven additional offices, a safe room and toilets were approved for the Education Department on the Bishop Street side of the Town Hall whilst the Borough Police took over practically the entire basement which resulted in considerable improvement in the cell and office accommodation. The alterations to the Town Hall were carried out by Messrs Haskard, Rudkin and Beck, Building Contractors, 35 Braunstone Gate, Leicester at a total cost of £6,550. The work was finally completed in 1910.

An important addition to the Town Hall Square came in 1909 with the ceremonial unveiling of the Leicestershire South African War Memorial. Leicester and the County had lost over 300 of its sons in the Boer War (1899 - 1902) and there was a strong desire, locally, for a permanent War Memorial to be erected in their memory. The Leicestershire South African War Memorial Committee was formed on 12 January 1903 with the specific task of raising the money and planning a suitable memorial.

The Town Council granted permission on 19 May 1903 for the proposed War Memorial to be erected at the entrance to Victoria Park. Initially, the eminently known Sir Alfred Gilbert (Professor of Sculptor, Royal Academy 1900 - 1909) was chosen as the sculptor for the War Memorial but endless delays were encountered and, in January 1908, the Committee's contract with Gilbert was cancelled. A local sculptor, Joseph Crosland McClure of the Leicester Municipal Art School, 51 The Newarke, was commissioned to undertake the work, the total cost of which was £1,355.

On 28 April 1909, the Corporation decided to abandon the original site on Victoria Park and granted permission for the War Memorial to be erected in the Town Hall Square fronting Horsefair Street. Following completion, the long-awaited unveiling ceremony took place on Thursday 1 July 1909 and was performed by Field Marshall Lord Grenfell, GCB, GCMG in

The unveiling of the Leicestershire South African War Memorial
(Leicester Mercury)

front of a huge gathering of people. The Leicestershire Regiment who lost 155 officers, NCOs and men in the Boer War provided a Guard of Honour comprised of a 100 strong contingent from the 1st Battalion of the regiment.

Alderman
Jonathan North JP
(Leicester City Council)

In the early 1930s the War Memorial was repositioned at the north east corner of Town Hall Square (its present site) during alteration work on the layout of the square.

Throughout the four harrowing years of the First World War, Leicester was well served by an exceptional public figure who held the office of Mayor for the entire period of the terrible conflict. Alderman Jonathan North, a Leicester born man, was a highly successful boot and shoe manufacturer who became the chairman and managing director of the huge firm of Freeman, Hardy and Willis in the town. The Mayor and Mayoress, Mrs Kate Eliza North gave, unstintingly, of themselves during a lengthy and demanding time in civic office.

On 28 June 1917, a temporary War Memorial was unveiled by the Duke of Rutland on the eastern side of Town Hall Square, facing the front entrance of the Town Hall itself. The memorial, which took the form of a screen wall and side panels, was designed by Samuel Perkins Pick, the Headmaster of the Leicester Municipal Art School and Benjamin John Fletcher, the Architect and Engineer to the Leicestershire County Council. The sculptor was Joseph Herbert Morcom of The Newarke, Leicester. The names of 2,129 Leicestershire men who had died, during the war, were inscribed on the memorial with space available for those who were to die later in the conflict. The cost of the temporary structure (£684.0s.0d) was met from the Mayor's Fund which Alderman North had launched in 1916 and was known as the "Mayors Fund for Disabled Warriors". The Mayor promised that a permanent War Memorial would be erected after the cessation of hostilities.

The promise made by Alderman Jonathan North was kept. Leicester's permanent War Memorial, designed by the eminent architect Sir Edwin Lutyens was duly erected on Victoria Park and unveiled on 4 July 1925.

Following the end of the First World War, Leicester was honoured by the visit of King George V and Queen Mary. His Majesty warmly thanked the people of Leicester for their stirling efforts: "In the important work of clothing and equipping our troops" during the titanic struggle and sacrifice which they had endured during the lengthy and distressing years of the war.

The Unveiling and Dedication of the Temporary War Memorial
(Leicester Mercury)

Alderman Jonathan North, whose long Mayoralty had been characterised by outstanding service and leadership, was knighted by the King, in the De Montfort Hall, on 10 June 1919.

Following the visit of the King, the restoration of the ancient title of City was accorded to Leicester on 19 July 1919. The Letters Patent were read out to a meeting of the Town Council, at the Town Hall, on 29 July by the Town Clerk, Herbert Arthur Pritchard.

The extract from the minutes of the Council read as follows:

The Town Clerk reads the following Letters Patent restoring to the town the title of City—

GEORGE THE FIFTH BY THE GRACE OF GOD of the United Kingdom of Great Britain and Ireland and of the British Dominions beyond the Seas King Defender of the Faith TO ALL TO WHOM THESE PRESENTS SHALL COME GREETING KNOW YE that we taking into consideration the antiquity and importance of our County Borough of Leicester of Our especial Grace certain knowledge and mere motion DO by this Our Royal Charter will ordain constitute declare and appoint that the said County Borough of Leicester shall henceforth for the future and for ever hereafter be a City and shall be called and styled "THE CITY OF LEICESTER" instead of the County Borough of Leicester and shall have all such rank liberties privileges and immunities as are incident to a City AND WE FURTHER DECLARE AND DIRECT that the Mayor Aldermen and Burgesses of our said County Borough of Leicester shall henceforth and by virtue of this Our Royal Charter be one body politic and corporate by the name and style of "THE MAYOR ALDERMEN AND CITIZENS OF THE CITY OF LEICESTER" with all such and the same powers and privileges as they have hitherto had as the Mayor Aldermen and Burgesses of the County Borough of Leicester and as if they had been incorporated by the name of the Mayor Aldermen and Citizens of the City of Leicester instead of the Mayor Aldermen and Burgesses of the Borough of Leicester.

IN WITNESS whereof We have caused these Our Letters to be made Patent WITNESS Ourself at Westminster the nineteenth day of July in the tenth year of Our Reign.

THE GREAT SEAL

BY WARRANT UNDER THE KING'S SIGN MANUAL.

At a meeting of the Leicester City Council, on 31 January 1922, it was reported that: "The Estate and Burial Grounds Committee has been urged by the Finance Committee to consider the provision of additional office accommodation at the Town Hall particularly as regards the Treasurer's Department." The offices, which were occupied by the general finance and audit staff, had become inadequate to house the level of staff required in the 1920s as Local Government services expanded.

Sketch plans were drawn up by the City Surveyor, Enoch George Mawbey, which provided for the building of a block of offices in Bowling Green Street "on the site of the existing mortuary, certain other buildings and adjoining land." It was agreed that an architect should be appointed: "To prepare the requisite plans, specifications etc. and that tenders be obtained."

A firm of local architects, Cowdell and Bryan, 8 New Street, Leicester was chosen to carry out the extension work to the Town Hall. Clearance and preparation of the site involved the demolition of the old mortuary, and the former house of the Head Constable plus the offices of the Sanitary and Building Inspectors. The new extension was designed to front Bowling Green Street and to link the two wings from Bishop Street to Horsefair Street. Importantly, the design was: "To correspond with the existing building linking the present building and forming a complete whole." The estimated cost of the work (excluding furniture and Architects' fees) was £35,750.

The extension to the Town Hall
(Derek Seaton)

Twenty one tenders were received and, on 24 April 1923, the quotation submitted by James Chapman and Sons Limited, Building Contractors, Knighton Junction, Welford Road, Leicester was accepted in the sum of £33,383.

The demolition of the old mortuary, prior to the building of the extension, finally enabled the Town Councillors to rid themselves of a source of controversy which had existed since 1893. This had arisen from occasional obnoxious smells, particularly in the summer months, coming from decomposing bodies in the mortuary, in close proximity to the police station and the homes of local residents. A temporary mortuary was set up, initially in 1923 at the disused fire station at the Aylestone Police Station situated in Lansdowne Road. Once again, complaints were received from people living nearby, and eventually, a new purpose-built Public Mortuary was opened on Welford Road close to Leicester's cattle market., It remained in use until 1961 when it became established at the Leicester Royal Infirmary.

The extension to the Town Hall was completed in 1925, whereupon an application was made to the Minister of Health for the sanction of a loan for the provision of fixtures, fittings and furniture in the sum of £4,350. One local firm contracted to undertake the fittings was R. Morley and Sons, 14 Cheapside, Leicester.

Meanwhile, Francis John Hames, the visionary architect who created Leicester's Town Hall almost half a century earlier, died at his home 14 Grays Inn Square, London on 28 May 1922 in his 73rd year.

A tribute to the Leicester born architect appeared in the *Leicester Daily Mercury* on Monday, 29 May 1922. He was described as: "One of the leading Architects in Leicester and his ability won for him the distinction of designing the present Town Hall which stands as a test to his undoubted gifts as a designer."

His funeral service was held, two days later, at the beautiful Parish Church of St Andrew, Holborn (rebuilt by Sir Christopher Wren 1684-86), followed by cremation at Golders Green Crematorium.

14 Grays Inn Square, London
(Derek Seaton)

St Andrew, Holborn
(Derek Seaton)

Alderman James Thomas
1927
(Leicester City Council)

An event of great importance in Leicester's civic history took place in 1928 during the Mayoral Year of Alderman James Thomas. His Majesty King George V graciously commanded that: "The Chief Magistrate now and for the time being of the City of Leicester shall be styled, entitled and called LORD MAYOR OF LEICESTER." Thus Alderman Thomas, the 470th individual Mayor since the initial holder of the position of chief citizen, William fil. Leveric, Alderman in 1209, became the first Lord Mayor of Leicester.

The Letters Patent under the Great Seal, granting the title, were dated 10 July 1928, and the City Council was required to pay a sum of £57 15s 6d in order to enable the Secretary of State to defray the various Stamp Duties and fees in connection with the preparation of the Letters Patent!

Further alterations to the interior of the Town Hall took place during 1931 and 1932. The implementation of a major scheme was approved by the Leicester City Council, on 30 June 1931, in order to improve the amenities available to the Lord Mayor and members of the Council, together with improvements in the departmental accommodation. The scheme was designed to provide a new Council Chamber, on the site of the then existing chamber, and a suite of offices for the Lord Mayor and Lady Mayoress plus a lounge and tearooms, for the Aldermen and Councillors, all located on the first floor.

Former Public Assistance Department's Offices, Pocklington's Walk, Leicester (Redfern & Sawday 1883) Now the offices of the Leicester Registration District, Leicester City Council (Derek Seaton)

The tender submitted by Henry Herbert and Sons, Building Contractors, 33 Millstone Lane, Leicester was accepted in the sum of £23,314. The City Surveyor, Thomas Gooseman assumed responsibility for the project. The work was carried out in three stages during an eighteen month period which necessitated the monthly Council Meetings being held in the Committee Rooms at the Public Assistance Department's Offices in nearby Pocklington's Walk.

The new Council Chamber measured 2405 square feet as compared with the former chamber, which was 1792 square feet in size, and was capable of accommodating 100 members of the Council and staff. The lounge and tearoom, an entirely new feature, was erected over the courts, whilst the suite of offices for the Lord Mayor and Lady Mayoress occupied a site which originally formed part of the Town Clerk's Department.

The new Council Chamber was formally opened by the Lord Mayor, Alderman Walter Ernest Wilford J.P. on 24 October 1932.

Alderman Walter Ernest Wilford J.P., Lord Mayor of Leicester 1931-32 (Leicester City Council)

Council Chamber (Leicester Mercury)

Lounge and Tearoom
(Derek Seaton)

Throughout the period 1876 to 1930 it was the custom of the City Council to place, in the former Council Chamber, an illuminated brass plaque bearing the name of each retiring Mayor or Lord Mayor. Prior to the construction of the new Council Chamber, it was necessary to remove the fifty-one plaques and attach them to the oak panelling in the waiting room between the Courts of Justice. Additional individual plaques were fixed to the panelling, each year, until all the available space was taken up. (The last plaque to be added was in respect of Alderman Miss May Goodwin, who was elected to the office of Lord Mayor on 26 May 1961). A total of 84 plaques commemorate those citizens of Leicester who held the office of Mayor or Lord Mayor between 1876 and 1961.

Provision was also made, in 1933, for the names of all of the Mayors and Lord Mayors, since the implementation of the Municipal Corporations Act 1835, to be entered, in gold lettering, on oak panels in the new Ante Chamber. Space was also made available "for the purpose for approximately the next one hundred years."

By 1928 the need for a larger and purpose-built headquarters for the Leicester City Police Force was recognised. A site was chosen in Charles Street and the building of the new police station commenced in the spring of 1932. The opening of the Charles Street headquarters took place on 4 September 1933 when the City's Police Force took possession of their new home after having been based at the Town Hall for a continuous period of 57 years.

During a twelve month time span between September 1938 and the outbreak of the Second World War, on 3 September 1939, intense activity was taking place at the Town Hall as Leicester prepared for the approaching conflict. Jack Collinson, then a very Junior Assistant who, after service in the Royal Air Force, eventually became Assistant Town Clerk and finally Assistant Chief Executive of the Leicestershire County Council, has clear recollections of that period. He recounts that, in early 1939, Town Hall staff, regardless of position or seniority, voluntarily undertook training as fire watchers or "Jim Crows" as Winston Churchill called them in readiness for anticipated German air raids upon the City. Issued with steel helmets, firemen's belts and axes, plus powerful torches, they patrolled the Town Hall roof nightly. They quickly became familiar with the building's many gables and gullies and accomplished the ascent of the clock tower by means of a precarious ladder positioned to pass through the actual workings of the clock itself.

Jack Collinson vividly recalls those anxious days and relates: "The Town Clerk himself, Laurence McEvoy, a solicitor of the 'old school' with a fund of pithy epithets for every situation, insisted on taking his turn on the rota. He proved to be a formidable opponent on the cribbage board, during off-duty hours, and was no mean performer on the ubiquitous dartboard!"

Within three days of war being declared work commenced on the construction of a trench type air raid shelter in Town Hall Square, situated at the Every Street end to the left of the temporary War Memorial. As the threat of enemy air raids drew ever closer, the City

The Town Hall on 20 November 1940 (Leicester Mercury)

Council agreed, on 28 November 1939, to make provision for an air raid shelter, in the basement of the Town Hall, for the use of 280 members of staff at a cost of £472.

On the night of 19 November 1940, the city suffered its most severe attack of bombing by enemy aircraft. During the "blitz" of Leicester, 108 people were killed and 208 were injured. There was considerable bomb damage caused to houses and business premises, particularly in the Highfields and Rutland Street areas, and one casualty of the air raid was the Town Hall. Jack Collinson recollects that a large high explosive bomb of about 1000 lb had penetrated the roof; it passed through the Town Planning Department on the second floor, the Lord Mayor's Secretary's Office on the first floor, the fire watchers off-duty room situated alongside the main entrance on the ground floor before reaching its final resting place in the basement without exploding. On each floor, through which the bomb passed, was a neat hole several yards square marking its downward route to the basement.

The bomb landed in a vertical position standing on its nose and neatly positioned beside one of the large gas meters. Upon close inspection, by the fire watchers, it was discovered that there was a split in the bomb casing through which the main filling of explosive material was spilling out. Water pressure, in the centre of the city, was low due to the many fires being fought in nearby buildings and the services of the Bomb Disposal Squad was stretched to the limit as they tried to cope with the severity of the attack which lasted for eight hours.

Next morning the bomb was made safe by the Bomb Disposal Squad and as Jack Collinson now reflects: "Perhaps the incident justifies some reflection on how Leicester would have looked today if the Town Hall had been blown up!" This was indeed a narrow escape for *Leicester's Victorian Jewel."*

The Council Chamber was the setting for a highly significant event in Leicester's civic history when, on 19 November 1941, Councillor Miss Elizabeth Rowley Frisby MBE became the first lady to be elected as Lord Mayor of the City. Miss Frisby, who had an outstanding record of public service both locally and nationally, fully merited her election as the City's chief citizen, a position which had previously only been occupied by men since its inception in 1209.

During the past 63 years, since 1941, ten other ladies have held the office of Lord Mayor of Leicester.

Councillor Miss Elizabeth Rowley Frisby MBE
Lord Mayor of Leicester 1941-42
(Leicester City Council)

Leicester City Council played its part during the wartime years. The gardens in Town Hall Square were converted into allotments for the growing of food and as a resource where local citizens could be taught how to grow their own vegetables.

Following the cessation of hostilities, Leicester was honoured by an official visit by Their Majesties King George VI and Queen Elizabeth on 30 October 1946. The visit was in response to a personal invitation by the Lord Mayor, Councillor Charles Edward Worthington to the King. During a busy day of engagements, the King and Queen were received at the Town Hall by the Lord Mayor, where they were the honoured guests at a luncheon hosted by Councillor Worthington.

At a meeting of the City Council on 27 July 1948 it was agreed, in principle, that a scheme involving a major reconstruction of Town Hall Square should go ahead. The scheme provided for a garden layout and for the removal of the temporary War Memorial and the Fountain. It was envisaged that the scheme would not be undertaken for some time as it would not be possible to obtain a permit for the finance and labour required.

During the Mayoralty of Alderman Thomas Rowland Hill, it was the sad duty of the Lord Mayor to read out the Proclamation declaring the death of King George VI on 6 February 1952 and the succession of Her Majesty Queen Elizabeth II. The ceremony took place in front of the Town Hall on Friday 8 February 1952. A detachment of one hundred soldiers

The Guard of Honour assembled outside the Town Hall for the reading of the Proclamation (Leicester Mercury)

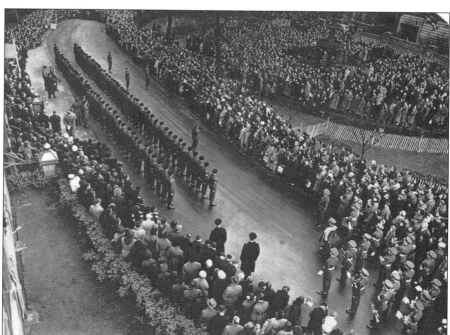

comprising of troops drawn from the Royal Leicestershire Regiment, stationed at their depot at Glen Parva Barracks, and 579 L.A.A. Regiment R.A. (The Royal Leicestershire Regiment) T.A., based at Ulverscroft Road Drill Hall, Leicester formed a Guard of Honour.

Taking part in that historic event were two young soldiers; one a future Lord Mayor of Leicester - 22435860 Private Wigglesworth R. (Lord Mayor 1992-93) and the other was the author - 22092608 Gunner Seaton D.

During the winter of 1954 a deputation from the Leicestershire and Rutland Branch of the British Legion (became the Royal British Legion in 1971) met with members of the Estate and Burial Grounds Committee to express their concern regarding the "deplorable condition of the temporary War Memorial in Town Hall Square." Some of the inscriptions were worn and almost indecipherable. It was accepted that the permanent War Memorial on Victoria Park had effectively taken the place of the temporary Memorial and that a Roll of Honour had been placed in the Cathedral Church of St Martin bearing the names of the fallen. The British Legion intimated that they had no intention of asking the Council to retain the temporary War Memorial. At a meeting of the City Council on 23 February 1954 the demolition of the temporary War Memorial was approved but, fortunately, there was no further mention of the earlier proposal to demolish the Fountain in Town Hall Square!

The Demolition of the temporary War Memorial 29 April 1954
(Leicester Mercury)

Her Majesty Queen Elizabeth II and His Royal Highness The Duke of Edinburgh visited Leicester for the first time, during the Queen's reign, on 9 May 1958. Whilst in the city, the Queen opened the Percy Gee building at the University of Leicester, toured the factory of N. Corah (St Margaret) Ltd and visited the De Montfort Hall. The final engagement was a visit to the Town Hall where the Lord Mayor, Alderman Frederick Jackson presented the Queen with an engraved silver Rose Bowl on behalf of the citizens of Leicester.

The Queen and the Duke of Edinburgh chatting to the Lord Mayor, Alderman Frederick Jackson and the Lady Mayoress, Councillor Mrs Constance Jackson outside the Town Hall (Leicester Mercury)

The silver Rose Bowl presented to the Queen (Leicester Mercury)

Staff risk life and limb to catch a glimpse of the Queen entering the Town Hall
(Leicester City Council)

On 21 May 1970 the imposing figure of the Leicester Wyvern which dominated the gable over the front entrance to the Town Hall was, seemingly, decapitated. The stone head and beak, weighing some 30 lb, crashed on to the roof of the building and then fell over sixty feet on to the bonnet of a parked Rover 2000 car, which belonged to the Clerk of the Peace, Stanley Whait. He was in attendance in one of the courts at the time and returned to find his prized vehicle "badly battered".

The entire facade of the Town Hall had been inspected, after cleaning operations, just prior to the incident and no signs of weakness had been detected in the Wyvern's structure. A passer-by suggested that the speeches at the previous night's Mayor-making Ceremony, when Alderman George Ernest Baldwin was elected as Lord Mayor, "had brought the house down!"

The architectural importance and historical significance of the Town Hall and its surroundings was recognised, on 30 March 1972, when the building was given Grade II* listed status. This was followed, on 14 March 1975, when both the Fountain in Town Hall Square and the Leicestershire South African War Memorial were accorded Grade II listing.

Alderman Herbert Stanley Tomlinson
Lord Mayor of Leicester 1972-3
(Leicester City Council)

During the Mayoralty of Alderman Herbert Stanley Tomlinson (1972-73), Parliament passed the Local Government Act 1972. The Act, which was due to come into force on 1 April 1974, radically changed the face of Local Government and resulted in Leicester being deprived of its status as a County Borough. The City became a District Council and lost responsibility for a number of its major services to the new Leicestershire County Council. The Act also abolished the historic office of Alderman, thus Alderman Tomlinson became the last Alderman to serve as Lord Mayor of Leicester.

The title of Lord Mayor was, however, preserved by a grant from her Majesty Queen Elizabeth II approving the use of the title by the Chairman of the new Leicester District Council.

The arrow points to the headless
Wyvern on 22 May 1970
(Leicester Mercury)

Chapter Three:
Centenary and beyond

Leicester's Town Hall reached its centenary in August 1976. In November of that year, Professor Jack Simmons who was Professor of History at the University of Leicester addressed a meeting of the Leicestershire Archaeological and Historical Society at the Guildhall. Speaking on the history of Francis Hames' 1876 civic building, Professor Simmons remarked that "Leicester achieved one of its rare visual distinctions when the Town Hall was built 100 years ago." He went on say: "It only had one peer among the public buildings of its time, and that is not a Town Hall but the Harris Library and Museum in Preston." A rare accolade indeed.

Workmen tightening the
Town Hall Bells 1976
(Leicester Mercury)

During December 1976, remedial work was carried out on the Town Hall clock and the clock tower. A firm of specialists from Derby was commissioned to tighten the bells, in their struts, and synchronise them with the clock hands. The overhaul also included work on the timbers, which were found to have rotted, and securing the weather vane which had worked loose. The total cost of the remedial work amounted to £700 which was only £207 less than the accepted tender for making and installing the timepiece a century earlier.

In addition, further work was carried out on the fountain in Town Hall Square. Until 1970 water for the fountain came from the mains. In order to avoid waste a change to a circulatory system was introduced but it was only in December 1976 that the system was adapted to include the spray effects.

"This one has got to come out!" A caption which appeared with the unusual and amusing photograph in the Leicester Mercury dated 7 December 1976. The workman, with what appeared to be a pair of pliers, about to perform an extraction, was Roy Ingram who was actually tightening up a valve in the mouth of one of the winged lions featured on the fountain. The result was that the four lions could spray water again for the first time in six years.

During 1975 the City Council considered the need to centralise its administration. An interest was taken in two independent office blocks, one of fourteen storeys and one of nine storeys, erected by a developer at nearby Welford Place. The twin tower office block, known as the New Walk Centre, was eventually acquired by the Council and the following year staff from the various departments moved into the new administrative complex. The Town Hall remained as the City's civic headquarters.

Four years later, in 1980, the Crown Court (formerly the Assize Courts - abolished by the Courts Act 1971), which had been held at the Town Hall since 1876, moved to the new Crown Court, built by the Birmingham Regional office of the Property Services Agency, in Wellington Street, Leicester.

"This one has got to
come out!"
(Leicester Mercury)

The Queen with Richard and David Scott accompanied by the Lord Mayor, Councillor William Scotton, the boys' grandfather (Leicester Mercury)

The Queen with the Lord Mayor, at the commencement of the Royal walkabout, in front of the Town Hall (Leicester Mercury)

A second visit to Leicester was made by the Queen and the Duke of Edinburgh on 14 March 1980. During a busy day of engagements, Her Majesty and Prince Philip again visited the Town Hall where the Lord Mayor, Councillor William Henry Scotton addressed the royal visitors at a Civic Reception before assembled dignitaries and guests.

As the Queen left the Members' Tea Room, after signing the distinguished visitors' book, she had a special smile for the two youngest guests in the room, Richard aged 13 years and David Scott aged 10, the two sons of the Lady Mayoress, Mrs Helen Scott.

Huge crowds gathered to welcome Her Majesty and Prince Philip and, despite the inclement weather, the Queen, together with the Lord Mayor, carried out the eagerly anticipated walkabout from the Town Hall to the Clock Tower in the heart of the City.

Increasingly, over the years, the Town Hall Square showed marked signs of wear and deterioration. In 1987 consideration was given by the City Council to the redesigning of the Square and a programme of restoration was agreed at a cost of £211,000. The work included improvements to provide an open space with an elegant paved forecourt in front of the Town Hall bearing a mosaic of the City's Coat of Arms created by the Leicestershire

firm of Ibstock Brick. Railings with lion finials were added to compliment the Victorian architecture of the Town Hall and surrounding buildings.

The re-creation of the Town Hall Square, in order to highlight its original Victorian splendour, was reopened by Her Royal Highness the Duchess of Kent on 11 July 1989.

A new decade saw the removal of the Magistrates' Courts from the Town Hall following the building of the new Courthouse in Pocklington's Walk. The new Magistrates' Courts were formally opened by the Lord Chancellor, the Right Honourable the Lord MacKay of Clashfern on 13 November 1992.

The Duchess of Kent accompanied by the Lord Mayor Councillor David Taylor at the reopening (Leicester City Council)

Eugene Dowds pictured with the City's collection of Maces
(Leicester Mercury)

In July 1993, the popular tours of Leicester's Town Hall commenced. Eugene Dowds became the first official guide of the City's major public building. He had commenced working at the Town Hall, as a caretaker and night watchman, in 1957, a post he was to hold for 44 years until his retirement in 2001.

He acquired an enormous fund of knowledge about the Town Hall, took many excellent photographs of the building and entertained groups of visitors, on the first Wednesday of each month, on free public tours together with tours arranged for other guests by appointment. His ready wit and unmistakable North Ireland accent made him a popular and well-known local figure. Sadly, Eugene died in February 2002. Many of the photographs in this book were taken by Eugene and serve as a lasting tribute to someone who had a real passion for the building in which he worked for four decades.

Eugene is holding a replica of a Great Mace. The replica is 117 centimetres long, silver gilt and is dated Birmingham 1913. It was presented to the Corporation of Leicester in January 1914 by John Breedon Everard, High Sheriff of Leicestershire. This is the mace currently in use on civic occasions.

The three maces in the glass case complete a unique collection and are comprised of: in the foreground the small Lincoln Mace, a 30 centimetre silver mace with the Royal Arms and supporters upon the head. It was presented to the Town of Leicester by King Charles I in 1641 and later sold with the civic regalia and plate at a public auction in 1836. Subsequently, it was purchased by a Lincoln silversmith who bequested it to the City of Lincoln. In 1935, Lincoln released the tiny mace on permanent loan to the City of Leicester and it has remained with the Leicester civic regalia and plate to this day.

Immediately behind the Lincoln Mace is a 50 centimetre silver and silver gilt ceremonial mace with gilt head dated 1650. The silver staff was replaced circa 1780. The ceremonial mace, having been sold, was later repurchased by the Town Council.

At the rear of the case is a silver gilt mace approximately 110 centimetres in length, purchased by the Corporation in 1649. This was a replacement for the Great Mace stolen by the Royalists during the siege of Leicester in 1645. It was sold at auction in 1836 and, eventually, repurchased by public subscription in 1866.

The Town Hall tours continue to take place on the first Wednesday of each month and are ably led by two local Blue Badge Guides.

On 1 April 1997, Councillor Culdipp Singh Bhatti was privileged to be Lord Mayor of Leicester when the City acquired Unitary Status and the return of its major services after a lapse of twenty three years. The Lord Mayor attended a ceremony on the appointed day, when he was presented with the original Silver Key to the Town Hall entrance gates.

The key was the one used by Alderman William

Councillor Bhatti opening the Town Hall gates on 1 April 1997 (Leicester City Council)

Barfoot, Mayor of Leicester 1875/76, to open the Town Hall on Monday 7 August 1876. Sixty five years later, in 1941, the key was purchased by the then Lord Mayor, Alderman William Joseph Cort from the son of the late Alderman Barfoot and handed back to the Corporation. Members of the Council expressed their appreciation of the generosity of the Lord Mayor and placed the key in the custody of the Museum and Libraries Committee.

Councillor Bhatti duly opened the gates with the restored key, which was first used to open the Town Hall 120 years earlier, to mark the historic occasion.

At the present time the Town Hall serves a variety of purposes. The monthly meetings of the Leicester City Council continue to be held in the Council Chamber which is also used for the Annual Meeting of the Council and Election of the Lord Mayor which takes place in May. The Council Chamber is also used, on occasions, when the Honorary Freedom of the City is bestowed upon worthy individuals.

The Lord Mayor's Office and Secretariat are located on the first floor and the former Court Room 1 is currently used for Coroner's Inquests. Some of the accommodation in the building is occupied by Council staff and other offices are used by those involved in the work of the Twinning Associations

Plans are in hand for the two former court rooms to become the City's new civic wedding venues. It is envisaged that the magnificent interior of Court Room 1 will remain unaltered, it will, therefore, continue to be used as a room for larger Coroner's Courts and also as a room licensed for the conduct of civic weddings. Court Room 2 (originally the Nisi Prius Court) will probably be transformed although some of the original features are likely to stay. Other rooms will be utilised to house the staff and offices of the Registration District of the City Council, currently located in nearby Pocklington's Walk.

Leicester's Town Hall with its beautiful square and fountain continues to captivate both local people and visitors alike as it has done for the past 128 years. It symbolises the splendour of 19th century Leicester and remains a much-loved *Victorian Jewel* in the heart of the City.

The last word should go, appropriately, to Professor Jack Simmons who said in 1976: "How informal it is, warm in its mellowed red brick - not a showpiece but a domestic building more refined than all around it, yet of the same family. It is like an old and dignified smiling friend."

Bibliography

Banner, John W.
Discovering Leicester: the researches of a Leicester City Guide
Leicester 1991

Beazley, Ben
Peelers to Pandas: An Illustrated History of the Leicester City Police
Derby 2001

Cavanagh, Terry & Yarrington, Alison
Public Sculpture of Leicestershire and Rutland
Liverpool 2000

Hartopp, Henry
Roll of The Mayors and Lord Mayors of Leicester 1209 to 1935
Leicester 1936

Edited by Hinks, John
Aspects of Leicester
Barnsley 2000

Pegden, N.A.
Leicester Guildhall
Leicester 1981

Simmons, Jack
Leicester: The Ancient Borough to 1860
London 1974

Storey, John
Historical Sketch
Leicester 1895

Anderson, John
Leicester's Battle Against Fire
Blaby, Leics 1982

Wilshere, Jonathan
The Town Halls of Leicester
Leicester 1976

Other Sources:

- Minutes of the Leicester City Council
- *Leicester Advertiser*
- *Leicester Chronicle and The Leicestershire Mercury*
- *Leicester Daily Mercury*
- *Spencer's Illustrated Leicester Almanack 1877*

Appendix

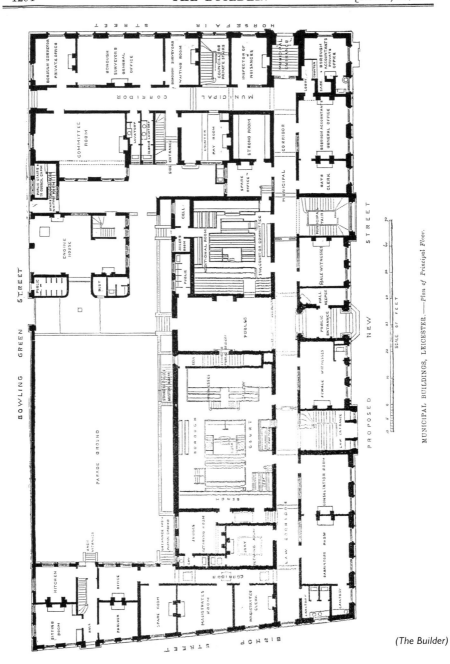

MUNICIPAL BUILDINGS, LEICESTER.—*Plan of Principal Floor.*

(The Builder)

Index